GUIDE TO

THE
REAL ALCÁZAR
OF
SEVILLE

Ana Marín Fidalgo

Legal deposit: 46983-1998
I.S.B.N.: 84-8003-128-X
Coordination: ALDEASA
Layout: Alberto Caffaratto
Translation: Nigel Williams
Photographs: Covadonga de Noriega
Photomechanical production: Lucam

Cover Illustration: Seville, Girault de Prangy
Printed in Spain by: Estudios Gráficos Europeos

(Printed in Spain)

CONTENTS

View of the Alcázar.

INTRODUCTION

The **Real Alcázar** ("Royal Palace-Fortress") is Seville's oldest and most historic palace complex. Since ancient times, each age has left its mark on this, Seville's foremost civil building, fashioning an extremely beautiful palimpsest on which the flux of time and history can be read. The visitor is therefore surprised first and foremost by its rich variety and multiplicity – second only to the harmonious balance of the whole and the relationship between parts governed by a very special beauty.

The Alcázar covers a large area in that part of Seville which has the greatest number of ancient buildings and monuments: it stands near the cathedral with its extremely beautiful tower – the Giralda – and is close to the General Archive of the Indies and the old Tobacco Factory (now a university). A few yards away lie the Arenal district and the River Guadalquivir, next to which, like a sentry at attention, stands the Alcázar's advance guard in this area – the Torre del Oro. The palace walls separate it from the beautiful Santa Cruz neighbourhood, a centre of attraction for local people and tourists alike.

The construction of this monumental group of buildings began in the early Middle Ages (913-914), while during the Renaissance and Baroque periods it was enhanced with the essential features of its present physiognomy, its wisely planned architecture having adapted to the needs imposed on it by each age – fragile Arabic forms, Gothic (and therefore Christian) austerity, the elegance and harmony of the classical and the fantasy of the Baroque. All in alliance to fashion the serene beauty of the Alcázar's courts, bedrooms, halls and gardens –

The Patio de las Banderas.

The wall facing the Plaza del Triunfo.

witnesses of historic events, and settings for legends and works of literature.

Through its rooms have filed such regal figures as Al-Mutadid and his son Al-Mutamid, St Ferdinand of Castile, Alfonso X the Wise, Peter the Cruel, Isabella the Catholic Queen, the Emperor Charles (who celebrated his marriage to the Infanta Isabella of Portugal here), Philip the Prudent... Austrias and Bourbons, intellectuals and politicians such as Ibn Handis the Sicilian, Boscán and Garcilaso, Navagiero and Baldassare Castiglione, Pablo de Olavide and Bruna, and discoverers of new worlds and sea routes, such as Christopher Columbus and Ferdinand Magellan: a host of figures whose presence has made this unique complex even more interesting.

Almost from the time of its origin with Al-Mutadid, the Alcázar was intended to serve as a Royal House and pavilion, and it has, in fact, continued to do so until the present time. Indeed, on 18th March 1995 the building became the setting for the celebration held on the occasion of the marriage of the king of Spain's elder daughter, the Infanta Elena de Borbón y Grecia, to Jaime de Marichalar, when the old walls welcomed the members of the Spanish royal family and representatives of other royal houses from all over Europe, thus making the palace and Seville the centre of attention for a number of days.

Since 24th April 1931 the complex has belonged to the Seville City Council, although in an agreement signed on 18th April 1988 by the Mayor of Seville and the Chairman of the "Board of Trustees of the National Heritage", it was established that the *Cuarto Real Alto* ("Upper Royal Chambers") and its adjacent areas were to be reserved

The Patio del Crucero in the Palacio de Al-Muwarak (Headquarters of the Consejería de Ordenación Territorial. Plaza de la Contratación).

indefinitely for the sole use of the Kings of Spain and members of the royal family whenever they visited the city. On such occasions the National Heritage takes possession of the Alcázar and it becomes a royal residence.

Since then an appointee of the Board of Trustees who attends to the management and conservation of the buildings and gardens (which belong to the Seville City Council), and a "National Heritage" representative who is responsible for their property and the contents of the upper palace and also manages the Historical Archive, are permanently on the premises.

I. ORIGINS

Since the earliest times the area within which the Real Alcázar of Seville stands has been one of great vitality. In Roman times it lay outside the city walls, its limits being the Guadalquivir (with its tributary the Tagarete), a branch of the Vía Augusta, its own outbuildings, and the city walls themselves. Here also lay the port and mercantile forum, thus making it an important centre for trade.

During the early-Christian era (426) a basilica dedicated to St Vincent the protomartyr was built in this area. Subsequently St Isidore of Seville served here and on his death was buried inside the basilica. Furthermore, according to records, Leander and his disciples also worked within its walls. The site of this building was probably a kind of small acropolis delimited by a wall and therefore outside the Visigothic *Spalis*. During the 1970s the remains of the basilica and its baptistry were excavated and studied, and may now be seen to the left of the Patio de las Banderas entrance.

II. THE MUSLIM PERIOD

According to Ibn al-Quitiyya, after the Muslims conquered the Iberian peninsula, emir Abd ar-Rahman III erected the Dar al-Imara ("House of the Governor") on the remains of the ancient basilica (913-914). What now remains of this small fortress designed by the Syrian Abdallah ben Sinan are: the parade ground, now the Patio de las Banderas; the old entrance gate, now walled-up but still visible in Calle Joaquín Romero Murube (leading to Plaza de la Alianza); and, finally, the walls, whose strong stone façade extends to the Plaza del Triunfo. These formed the original centre and are the oldest part of the Alcázar as it stands today.

The group of buildings probably stood apart from the city, covering the area between the Santa Cruz district and the Patio de la Montería in the Alcázar itself.

This fortification was the residence of the Banu Hachchach, great lords of Seville and the caliphate of Córdoba's representatives in the city. However, after the fall of the caliphate and during the *Taifa* period, the Abbadid king Al-Mutadid and his son Al-Mutamid lived here, the former a monarch who, feared yet admired, succeeded in making Seville the capital of the most prosperous kingdom in the peninsula. He was also an extraordinary poet who, during his reign, made Seville a great centre of poetry.

By this time (11th century), the original enclosure had become too small to meet the needs of such a complex court and so the walls were extended towards the west, where the **Puerta de Jerez** ("Door of Jerez") now stands, and a new, much more intricate and complete group of palace buildings called Al-Muwarak (meaning "the Blessed", or "the Palace-Fortress of the Blessing") sprang up.

In front of this stood a military esplanade which served as a parade ground for the old Bad al-Faray, now the Puerta de Jerez; its main access point faced the river and the door and stood within the small archway once called "La Plata" ("The Silver"), and now known as the "Miguel de Mañara". Another door opened onto what is now the **Patio del León** ("Court of the Lion"), which has always been a military compound in front of the palaces.

The Patio del Yeso.

This palace, whose living quarters lay around a garden with high walkways and rectangular pools, was later converted into the **Jardín del Crucero** ("Garden of the Crossing"); today its remains, unearthed and restored by the architect Rafael Manzano, can be seen in the court of the *Consejería de Obras Públicas y Transportes* in Plaza de la Contratación. On this site, the *Casa de la Contratación de las Indias* or "House of Trade with the Indies" was built in the 16th century.

Particularly important among the buildings belonging to this ancient palace was the **Salón del Trono** ("Throne Room"). Square in shape, it has a domed roof and stands apart from the other buildings; in Arabic documents it is referred to as "al-Turayyā", that is the "Room of the Pleiades". Three centuries later Peter I the Cruel was to make this magnificent, extremely beautiful room the **Salón de Embajadores** ("Hall of Ambassadors") and it became an extremely important part of his Mudéjar palace. Here Al-Mutamid presided over literary gatherings attended by court poets at which he himself would sing of his yearning for his beloved Rumaykyya and their passionate love whose matchless setting was this splendid palace.

The 12th century saw the beginning of another important period for the Alcázar – the Almohad period (1147-1237), during which Seville became the capital of the new North African empire. It was then when so many important and emblematic Sevillian buildings were constructed, among them the Great Mosque and its very beautiful minaret, the Giralda. But, as regards the area we are discussing, particularly important was a new military

Detail from the Patio del Yeso.

compound facing south whose triangular shape was delimited by a new wall beginning at the old Dar al-Imara. In time this was to become the area of the Alcázar's oldest gardens.

During this period a palace was also built as the official residence of Abu Yaqub Yusuf and Abu Yusuf Yaqub al-Mansur, the kings of this line. It had an extremely beautiful garden whose name became the **Baños de Doña María de Padilla** ("Baths of Doña María de Padilla"), when, in the middle of the 13th century, a **Gothic Palace** was raised on the remains of the building as a residence for Peter the Cruel's beautiful mistress.

Nearby, and probably forming part of this Almohad palace, one of the Alcázar's most beautiful courts was built; fortunately the **Patio del Yeso** ("Court of Stuccowork"), whose elegant composition and decoration are regarded as the direct forerunners of the Nasrid architecture of Granada, still stands.

III. THE ALCÁZAR BETWEEN THE 13TH AND 19TH CENTURIES

In 1248, when the King of Castile, Ferdinand III the Saint, wrested the city of Seville from the Muslims, the Alcázar became the residence of the Christian kings; since then it has always belonged to the kingdom of Castile. The courts, gardens, fountains, pools and ponds of the Muslim palaces were to have an extraordinary effect on the king, who had grown accustomed to the austere walls of Castilian monasteries. Ferdinand spent

Detail from the Patio del Yeso.

long periods here and when he died in the palace on 30th May 1252, he was buried in the royal chapel of Seville cathedral.

His son Alfonso X the Wise chose Seville as the capital of his kingdom, building a new palace to accommodate his court. Thus in the mid-13th century, Alfonso took advantage of the remains of the Almohad palace to have a building constructed in the Gothic style then in fashion. According to mediaeval records, this was known as the **Cuarto del Caracol** ("Room of the Spiral Staircase") and it was to become the symbol of Christian victory over Islam. Dominated by the old **Jardín del Crucero** ("Garden of the Crossing"), it stood on a rectangular plan with towers at each of its four corners containing the spiral staircases which gave it its name. The building consisted of four halls preceded by a gateway; two were large and ran parallel to the garden, while the other two, which were smaller, lay at right angles to the garden on either side of the larger ones. This building in now known as the **Salones de Carlos V** ("Halls of Charles V") and faces the **Court** and **Garden of Doña María de Padilla** (named after Peter the Cruel's mistress, whom Peter was madly in love with). Here also the intellectual court of Alfonso the Wise met in a place whose beauty inspired the king to write his *Cantigas* or "Ballads".

In 1340, the Alcázar was further enhanced by a new construction which shone with what is called the "Mudéjar" style in a combination of Christian and Islamic architectural elements. This was the **Sala de la Justicia** ("Room of Justice"), haughtily dominated by the **Patio del Yeso** and built by Alfonso XI after his victory at the Battle of Río Salado. These chambers were the

The Sala de la Justicia or Sala del Consejo.

setting not only for the king's love affair with the most beautiful lady of the Spain of those times, Leonor de Guzmán, but, years later, witnessed the murder of Master Fadrique on the orders of Peter the Cruel. It was Peter who ordered the Mudéjar palace known as the **Palacio del Rey Don Pedro** ("Palace of King Peter") – the focal point of the Alcázar as it is today – to be built. It was raised between 1364 and 1366, the craftsmen who worked on it including master builders and carpenters of Muslim origin, some from Seville, others from Granada and Toledo.

For the project Peter the Cruel asked his friend Mohammed V of Granada to send him courtiers capable of reproducing in Seville the delicate decoration and beautiful designs achieved in the splendid palace on the hill of the Alhambra. This is why in this royal residence in Seville we find designs, compositions, forms and lines which take us back to Nasrid Granada, to the caliphate of Córdoba, to Jewish and Muslim Toledo and to Almohad Seville; in other words it is a compendium of the best of Spanish Islamic, Andalusian Arabic and eastern architecture in general, sprinkled with mediaeval Christian architectural elements.

This old palace, which has reached us intact, was renovated and extended by the Spanish monarchs in order to adapt it, as the royal residence, to the needs of each new age. Thus, from the time of the Catholic Kings and throughout the centuries of Habsburg rule in Spain, another palace was built above it, giving rise to the **"Lower**

The Gothic Palace. The Hall next to the gardens.

summer house-upper winter house" concept, by means of which the palace was enlarged and, above all, conditions of comfort were improved in accordance with the requirements of each age.

Some of the areas around it, including courts, access points and outbuildings, were tidied up, so adding an even greater air of distinction to the palace. Furthermore, what are now the oldest **gardens** – a jewel of garden design from the reign of the Austrias – were created and laid out. During the 16th and 17th centuries the Alcázar took on its final form and, despite the inevitable wear and tear that comes with the passing of time, it has remained virtually unchanged ever since.

In the 18th century, when the Bourbons came to the Spanish throne, the Alcázar continued to be a stage for historic events, as, for example, the removal of the court to Seville, when Philip V and Isabella Farnese and their children took up residence there for five years (1729-1733). Although, in the 18th century, the main work carried out on the palace was of repair, maintenance and reinforcement, particularly after the disastrous Lisbon earthquake in 1755, some new buildings were added in the area of the old **Gothic Palace** and the **Patio de Doña María de Padilla,** (precisely because of the earthquake).

Since then no great changes have been made to the Alcázar. Restoration work has been carried out, on some occasions with little respect for the history of the complex, such as that undertaken in the 19th century during the reign of Isabella II, when moulds made from the stucco decoration in the Alhambra in Granada were used for the mezzanine floor and the gallery of the **Patio de las Muñecas** and most of the stuccowork in the palace was painted in loud colours.

IV. THE ALCÁZAR TODAY

In the course of this century a great deal of restoration, maintenance and conservation work has been carried out on the Alcázar. Particularly important in this respect was the creation of the **New Gardens** in the area of the old **Huerta del Retiro** ("Garden of Withdrawal"), thanks to which the Alcázar continues to maintain its splendid beauty and vitality.

Although the Alcázar is still a royal residence, it nevertheless serves other functions which have enabled it to move with the times and meet present-day social and cultural needs.

For example, it has become an extension of the City Council as a cultural centre for Seville, serving as a venue for exhibitions, concerts, plays, conferences and other activities connected with culture and entertainment.

But first and foremost it is a monument which each year draws large numbers of tourists interested in its extremely rich history, the great beauty of its architecture or simply the peace and quiet of its lovely gardens. Which is why in December 1987 Unesco declared it a **World Heritage** site.

View of the façade of the Palacio del Rey Don Pedro.

The desire on the part of the Alcázar's present owner, the Seville City Council, to bring the complex closer to the general public so that it can be admired by all, means that almost all its areas, buildings and gardens may now be visited. Moreover, in order to further promote the palace complex, the City Council, at a plenary meeting held on 31st July 1993, established the **Board of Trustees of the Real Alcázar** to lay down the guidelines for the management and conservation of the Alcázar – a step that has proved to be very positive for the maintenance of this unique complex.

THE VISIT

I. THE PUERTA DEL LEÓN

The main entrance to the complex, the Puerta del León ("Door of the Lion") is situated in the old Muslim wall (11th century) facing the Plaza del Triunfo and the cathedral. The name is a reference to the ceramic heraldic lion surmounting the door – a mediaeval symbol of royalty bearing a cross and a sash with the Latin inscription *Ad Utrunque* ("To be prepared for all") in a reference to Virgil's *Aeneid*. As this section of wall ran west (towards the Puerta de Jerez – the "Door of Jerez"), it encircled the Abbadid palace complex known as the Alcázar Al-Muwarak ("Blessed Fortress", 11th century) and to the east (towards the Santa Cruz district) delimited the first fortified enclosure and the Alcázar's oldest point, the Dar al-Imara ("House of the Governor", 10th century).

Detail from the Puerta del León.

The Puerta del León.

The doorway opens onto what is now known as the **Patio del León** ("Court of the Lion"). On the left-hand side of the entrance are the offices where tickets can be obtained for the visit to the Alcázar complex.

(Left) The Sala de Justicia or Sala del Consejo.

(Right) Detail from the stuccowork in the Sala de la Justicia.

II. THE PATIO DEL LEÓN

This is the first court in the Alcázar. Although it now has an elegant garden – the work of Juan de Talavera y Heredia, works manager when Joaquín Romero Murube was curator – it was originally a military esplanade in front of the palace. It is delimited by the Alcázar's outer walls and separated from the second court – the Patio de la Montería – by another, very old, section of wall whose three doorways provide a fine view of the extremely beautiful façade of the Mudéjar palace.

III. THE SALA DE LA JUSTICIA OR SALA DEL CONSEJO AND THE PATIO DEL YESO

This room is situated to the left of the Patio del León. It was built by Alfonso XI after his victory at the Battle of Río Salado (1340) on the site of the old Almohad palace (of which the extremely beautiful **Patio del Yeso** – "Court of Stuccowork", to which it leads, still stands). It has a square plan and its octagonal coffered ceiling is covered with very beautiful ornamentation. The walls contain niches with magnificent stucco decoration reminiscent of Toledo ornamentation. Particularly beautiful is the stuccowork over the archway leading to the Patio del Yeso (also known as the Patio de la Alberca – "Court of the Pool"), mentioned above; this still displays vestiges of its original delicate colouring. The new floor is of tile and brick and has at its centre a low marble fountain with a channel (also

The Sala de los Azulejos. The painting of the Entombment.

of marble) to take the water to the pool in the Court. According to legend Master Fadrique was murdered in this room by Peter I's henchmen.

Dating from the 12th century, the **Patio del Yeso** ("Court of Stuccowork") is not only one of the few remaining jewels of Sevillian Almohad architecture but also one of the few existing vestiges of the Muslim Alcázar. It is rectangular in shape and its novel and unusual layout was the immediate precursor of that used in the architecture of Granada. Particularly interesting is its gallery with three horseshoe arches resting on brick pillars and marble columns. In front of these rise openwork stucco decoration whose fragile forms are reflected in the waters of the pool in the centre of the court. In the 16th century all this area was occupied by the Cuarto del Maestre ("Room of the Master") and the Cuarto del Yeso ("Room of Stuccowork").

IV. THE SALA DE LOS AZULEJOS

To the right of the Patio del León stands what is now called the **Sala de los Azulejos** ("Room of the Tiles"). It contains a selection of remains of tiling and is, in fact, a small and extremely interesting museum of ceramics as its exhibits, dating from the 19th and 20th centuries (and belonging to the Seville City Council), came from a number of buildings and monuments. Also exhibited here is a 19th-century **canvas** depicting the **Procession of the Entombment,** belonging to the Seville City Council.

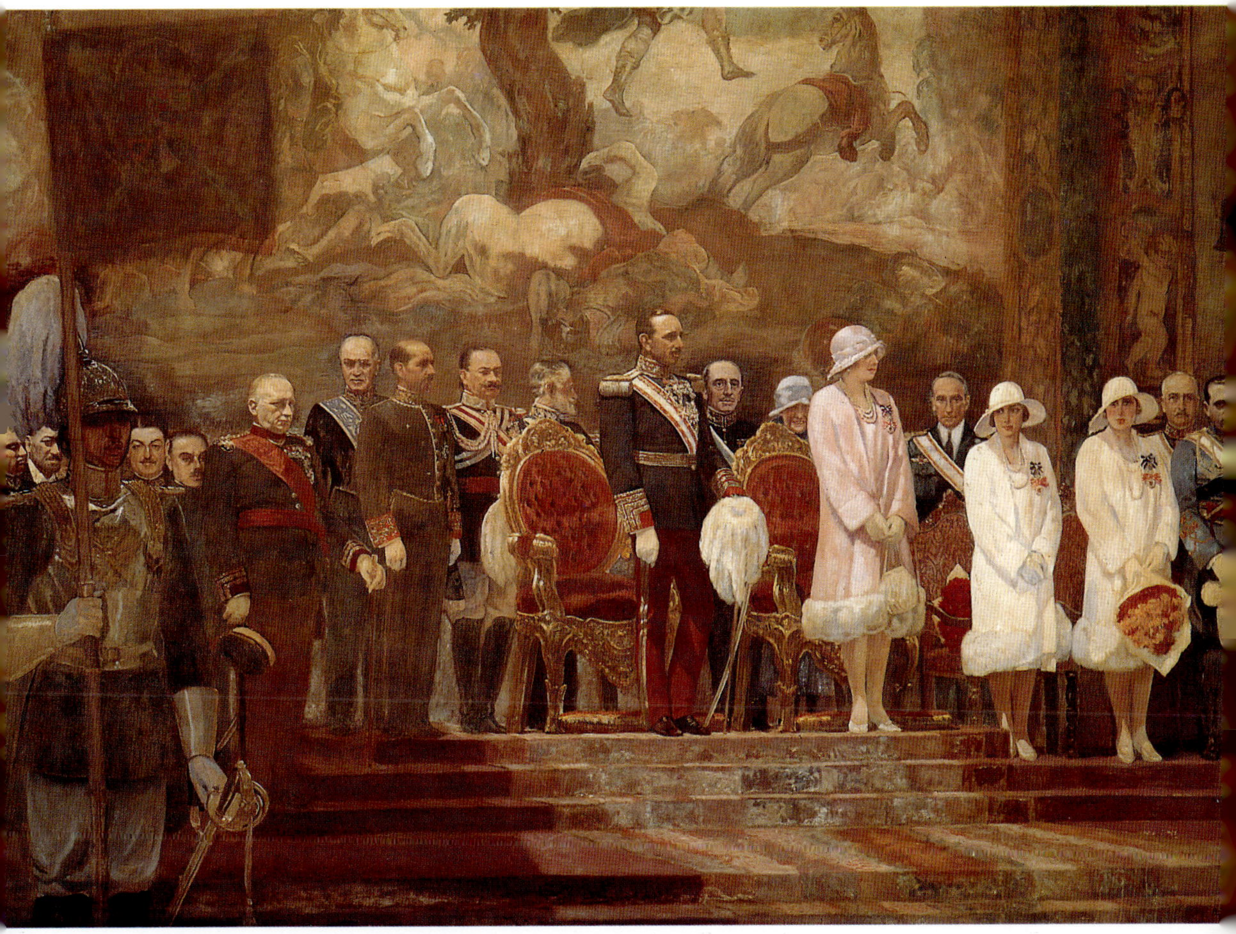

V. THE SALÓN DEL ALMIRANTE AND THE SALA DE AUDIENCIAS .... OF THE OLD HOUSE OF TRADE

The Salón del Almirante. Grosso's picture of The Inauguration of the Ibero-American Exhibition.

To the right of the Patio de la Montería are the rooms which formerly belonged to the old **Casa de Contratación de las Indias** ("House of Trade with the Indies"), established by the Catholic Kings in a decree of 14th January 1503. This area is of great historical importance as it was here where the plans were made for the very important enterprise which took the name and spirit of Spain to the new world.

In the 16th and 17th centuries these rooms formed what was known as the **Cuarto de la Montería** ("Room of the Hunt"). Our

The Salón de Audiencias (altarpiece of the Virgin of Navigators, Alejo Fernández).

description begins with the **Salón del Almirante** ("Hall of the Admiral"), a long, rectangular room with a wooden ceiling of horizontal beams resting on bases whose beautiful designs were inspired by those of Serlio. Dating from the late-16th century, this ceiling is ascribed to the Alcázar's head carpenter, who at that time was Martín Infante.

On the walls of this hall hang 19th- and 20th-century paintings belonging to the "National Heritage" and the Prado Museum. Of particular importance are the **portraits** of the **Duke and Duchess of Montpensier, The Death of Ferdinand III the Saint,** by Virgil Mattoni, and **The Inauguration of the Ibero-American Exhibition,** by Alfonso Grosso.

This room leads to what is known as the **Sala de Audiencias** ("Audience Room"), a square area with a rich painted and gilded 16th-century wooden ceiling decorated with geometric forms. On the walls are the coats of arms of a number of admirals important in Spanish naval history, the first, in chronological order, being Admiral Bonifaz, who accompanied St Ferdinand on the conquest of Seville in 1248. A rich Plateresque stucco frieze runs around the walls just below the ceiling. The room is dominated by the **altar and altarpiece of the Virgin of the Navigators** (16th century) by Alejo Fernández – the first picture painted in Europe on the subject of the discovery of America. It depicts Christopher Columbus, the Emperor Charles, Ferdinand the Catholic, Sancho de Matienzo (first treasurer of the House of Trade), Amerigo Vespucci, Juan de la Cosa and Indians from the newly discovered lands, all under the mantle of the "Virgin of Good Air". Below are the various types of craft which sailed to America, thus making this painting a record of incalculable value.

VI. THE PATIO DE LA MONTERÍA

From the **Salón del Almirante** a passage leads to the **Patio de la Montería** ("Court of the Hunt"). Built between 1584 and 1588, the passage was designed by the head mason Antón Sánchez Hurtado, who superposed semi-circular arches on marble columns, the lower ones being of the Tuscan order, the upper ones Ionic. Above these are iron balustrades dating from the same period. The glass covering is recent. The ceilings of both **galleries** date from the time of Martín Infante. Rather irregular in shape, the **court** stands in front of the Palacio del Rey Don Pedro, whose solemn, tapestry-like façade acts as a beautiful backdrop to it. To its left is a gallery similar to the one described, although this one was erected after the Lisbon earthquake of 1755 and at the same time as other buildings in the same area. The Patio de la Montería originally extended as far as the Puerta del León; it is said that here the king assembled his companions for the day's hunt.

VII. THE ROOMS AND COURT OF THE CUARTO DEL ASISTENTE

On the right at the back of the court a staircase leads to the upper **Cuarto Real** ("Royal Room"). To the side of this staircase a door in turn leads to a number of rooms called in the 18th century the **Cuarto del Asistente** ("Room of the *Asistente*") as the residence of the city's

The Patio del Cuarto del Asistente.

Asistente was there. In this context we must mention one man who was particularly important to Spanish culture and history and who once held the position of *Asistente*. This was Pablo de Olavide, famous for his literary gatherings and their ideas of the French Enlightenment. At the centre of this group of buildings lies the **court also known as that of the *Asistente*.** In the 17th century it contained the Alcázar's new kitchens and **offices,** built between 1614 and 1615 to plans by the Alcázar's master mason, the Milanese architect Vermondo Resta. This much restored court now has a Castilian air about it and contains the original marble columns from the lower gallery. A very cheerful, sunny court, it leads to other smaller ones such as those of the **Almirante** ("Admiral"), the **Mareantes** ("Navigators") and the **Levíes** ("Levites"), the first two alluding to the rooms they adjoin and the third to the extremely beautiful gallery above it, a gallery originally from the Palacio de los Levíes ("Palace of the Levites") in Seville and positioned here by the architect Rafael Manzano (who, in fact, laid out all this area).

In the 16th century the whole of this compound was known as the **Corral de las Piedras** ("Yard of Stones") as it was just that – a courtyard used for storing building materials.

An exhibition of ceramics has recently been set up here. The items on display, dating from the 16th to 19th century, belong to the Seville City Council.

VIII. THE PALACIO DEL REY DON PEDRO

This palace ("Palace of King Peter") was named after the king who erected it – Peter I of Castile, dubbed "the Cruel" and also "the Just". Built between 1364 and 1366, it emulates Muslim palaces like the Alhambra in Granada, those of the caliphate of Córdoba and the Almohad ones in Seville – all combined with elements and forms from Christian architecture. Its style, therefore, is Mudéjar. Although the name of the architect who designed it is not known, we do know that artists, master builders and craftsmen from Granada, Toledo and Seville took part in its construction. It is made up of two main areas, one a formal palace complex set out around the **Patio de las Doncellas** ("Court of the Damsels"), the other a more intimate area arranged around the **Patio de las Muñecas** ("Court of the Dolls").

A) The Façade

The palace façade stands at the back of the Patio de la Montería. To either side of the entrance are two-storey sections with semi-circular arches framed by mouldings. On the lower floor these arches stand on rectangular brick pillars. The upper floor displays a large central arch (also semi-circular) resting on pillars with vegetal motif

(Right) Detail.

(Left) The Palacio del Rey Don Pedro. The façade, central section.

(Below) Detail.

decoration above them. This is flanked on either side by groups of three small stilted semi-circular arches on small marble columns with Sevillian diamond-pattern panels above.

These **galleries** frame the windows of the upper palace's main halls and are adorned with stuccowork added after the conquest of

The Vestibule in the Palacio del Rey Don Pedro.

the kingdom of Granada – as is confirmed by the Granada heraldry adorning the depressions at the back and the fragile "Granada" appearance of the arches.

The extremely solemn **central section** of this façade is laid out like a beautiful tapestry, delimited at the sides by brick pillars resting on small marble columns. Above it project magnificent eaves of coloured pinewood – the renowned work of Toledo carpenters.

The lintel of the **doorway** in the centre of the lower section displays stone voussoirs carved with vine shoot motifs of Toledo origin, while the entrance itself is flanked by walled-up multifoil horseshoe arches, each resting on two small marble columns with diamond-pattern decoration above. Except for the bossage, which is more typical of Córdoba, these were executed in the local Almohad style. The ceramic curb around the panels on this façade reflect Oriental influence, while the small arches of straight and curved lines resting on small columns with pink and grey shafts are reminiscent of the designs used in 12th-century Sevillian architecture.

Granada is evoked in the relieving lintel, filled with blue and white tilework. Here the Nasrid motto is repeated: "And there is no victor but God". Castile is also present, however, in the characters of the inscription in monastic Gothic script framing the lintel. The inscription reads: *El muy alto y muy noble y muy poderoso y muy conqueridor D. Pedro, por la gracia de Dios Rey de Castilla y de León mandó fazer estos alcázares y estos palacios y estas portadas que fue hecho en la era de mil cuatrocientos y dos.* ("The very high and very noble and very powerful and very victorious Peter, King of Castile and of León by the grace of God, ordered this fortress and these palaces and these façades built, which was done in the year one thousand four hundred and two"). The date corresponds to the imperial era, that is to 1364 of the Christian calendar, when work on the palace began.

In its composition the whole of this façade recalls the Tower of Comares in the Alhambra; however, although larger, it is not nearly as exquisite.

B) The Vestibule

This is a long, narrow, rectangular room in three sections and connected with stilted semi-circular arches resting on columns surmounted with reused capitals. Three of these capitals are Visigothic and may have come from the old basilica dedicated to St Vincent that was discovered in what is now the Patio de las Banderas ("Court of the Flags"); the fourth was brought from the caliphate of Córdoba. The beautiful **ceiling** is decorated with painted interlacing ornamentation while around the walls runs a high stucco frieze of vegetal motif decoration, epigraphic inscriptions, scallops and stalactite-like decoration, all beautifully coloured. Set above geometric wall tiling is a **stucco frieze,** adorned

The façade of the Palacio del Rey Don Pedro.

with inscriptions in Muslim Kufic characters. This ornamentation covers every part of the arches – the extradoses, the archivolts and the intradoses. The modern paving is of Tarifa flags.

To the left and right of this small vestibule **exits** lead off at right angles to the main palace rooms. This arrangement was a feature

The Patio de las Doncellas. Detail from a tilework frieze.

common to almost all Muslim palaces and very much in line with the Oriental custom of maintaining one's privacy by impeding a direct view of a building's interior.

The **exit to the left** is a dark, narrow corridor which leads directly to the residential area of the palace, that is to the sovereign's most private apartments; its purpose was to ensure that in times of danger the monarch could leave quickly and out of sight of the court.

The exit on the right leads directly to the official area of the palace. It is a small, well-lit corridor whose most interesting features are doors of painted inlaid wood – the work of Toledo carpenters – and two vaults with Almohad designs. These vaults, which date from the 12th-century, prove that the construction work carried out during this period also affected this area and that previously existing structures were reused on the new palace. On the left along this corridor, a staircase leads up to the upper palace; in the old records it is referred to as the **Escaleras de Las Damas** ("Staircase of The Ladies").

C) The Patio de las Doncellas

The second door leads to the very beautiful and spectacular **Patio de las Doncellas** ("Court of the Damsels"), the old centre of the palace's official area. Standing on a rectangular plan, it is surrounded on its four sides by galleries, the lower ones formed by multifoil horseshoe arches, those in the middle being the largest and marking the court's main axes; all rest on extremely beautiful marble Corinthian columns made in the Renaissance workshops of the Aprille de Carona in Genoa to replace the original ones.

These arches are surmounted with diamond-pattern panels whose fine stucco decoration is reminiscent of Córdoba and Granada. Above these panels is a frieze framed by Muslim Kufic inscriptions in which the Nasrid motto "And there is no victor but God" is repeated again and again. In addition to its vegetal motif decoration this frieze displays the coats of arms of Castile, León and the imperial heraldry – the arms with the two-headed eagles and the pillars with the motto "Non plus ultra" – confirming that major alterations were made to the court in the 16th century.

The extremely beautiful tiled friezes with interlacing geometric forms, however, date from the Mudéjar period. All brightly-coloured and each one different, they bedeck the walls at the back of the galleries. The fabulous gilded and coloured doors of inlaid wood with small shutters bear a number of interlacing designs on both sides. Veritable masterpieces of Toledo carpentry, they lead to the main rooms that overlook the court. Without any doubt, the best of these belong to the **Salón de Embajadores** ("Hall of Ambassadors"), the most important room in this palace. Each bears an inscription with the year of its execution – 1366 –

View of the Patio de las Doncellas.

when, it is thought, the Mudéjar works in this area were completed.

Both the **corridors** and the centre of the **court** are paved with white marble, but during the 14th and 15th centuries the flooring was of tilework and clay slabs. The fountain in the centre is the original one.

Detail from the stuccowork decoration.

Window in the Dormitorio de los Reyes Moros.

The upper **galleries** were built after 1540 to plans by the royal architect Luis de Vega. Since the earliest period galleries had existed on the upper floor, probably with flat ceilings supported by brick pillars, although they were simpler than the present ones and so were replaced. The new ones are made up of semi-circular arches resting on marble Ionic columns and have turned balustrades, also of marble and from the Genoese workshops. Both the inner and outer **faces** were covered in Plateresque stuccowork. The present ones are the result of recent restoration carried out with moulds made from the remains of the old stuccowork in the south and west galleries. The face of the east corridor, which is completely covered with stucco decoration, is also the result of recent alterations; these have nothing whatever to do with the original building.

Despite the fact that major alterations were carried out on the court in the 16th century, the essential character of the Mudéjar construction was preserved; thus the new Classical elements combine perfectly with the old, mediaeval ones.

D) The Dormitorio de los Reyes Moros

The door in the centre of the right-hand gallery leads to this room, commonly known as the **Dormitorio de los Reyes Moros** ("Bedroom of the Moorish Kings"), although in the Mudéjar palace it was called the "Royal Room". It comprises two parallel rooms – the monarch's **Cámara Regia** ("Royal Chamber") and his **Dormitorio de Verano** ("Summer Bedroom").

The Dormitorio de los Reyes Moros.

Both rooms have a rectangular bedroom at the end, reached through horseshoe archways, the first displaying lambrequins, the second being a multifoil arch resting on marble columns whose pink shafts are surmounted with reused caliphal capitals. Also very Cordovan is the **archway** between the rooms – a triple arch on marble supports with capitals of the same kind as the previous ones and in all likelihood brought from Córdoba.

The stilted semi-circular **archway** leading into this room is surmounted with three openwork stucco latticed screens. The delicately coloured stucco decoration runs almost the whole length of the walls, surmounting and delimiting extremely beautiful tiled friezes with delightful geometric forms. The stuccowork is particularly profuse around the doors and arches, where it continues upwards.

The first of these rooms has small geminated windows with stilted semi-circular arches and small central columns with black shafts and Cordovan capitals. Also of great interest are the **ceilings,** particularly in the first room, where interlacing geometric shapes form extremely beautiful star-like formations and coffers in the form of a small vault resting on a frieze with the heraldry of the Castilian king, all in painted wood. The centre of the floor is paved with marble slabs flanked by zig-zagging clay and glazed tiles.

E) The Patio de las Muñecas

On the left, at the end of the Royal Chamber, an opening leads to the **Patio de las Muñecas** ("Court of the Dolls"), once the palace's main residential area. Before this, however, it is necessary to cross a small square room known as the **Cuadra de Pasos Perdidos** ("Hall of Lost Steps"). Here the flat ceiling, which dates from the time of the Catholic Kings, in all likelihood replaced the original panelled one when alterations were made in this area of the Upper Palace. The floor is of brick and tile. An opening on the left leads to the **Patio de las Doncellas.**

With good reason the Court of the Dolls can be considered one of the jewels of this palace. Indeed, with its small size, its extraordinary beauty and the sensitivity and meticulousness with which is was built, it could almost be regarded as a piece of gold

The Patio de las Muñecas. Detail from the stuccowork in the lower section.

The Patio de las Muñecas.

filigree. Its highly "Granadan" style is most evident in its stilted **semi-circular arches** and the asymmetry of its shorter walls. It is said that the columns, a combination of black and pink shafts surmounted with extremely delicate capitals in the taste of the caliphate, were brought to Seville from Córdoba by Al-Mutamid.

This **court** underwent a major transformation in the 19th century at the hands of the architect Rafael Contreras, who added a mezzanine with a historicist gallery above it, and a glass roof. The stucco ornamentation on these additions was made from moulds taken in the Alhambra in Granada. What therefore remains of the original work is to be found on the ground floor only.

According to local legend the name of this court comes from a number of **small heads** in the base of the left arch in the north gallery. The entire floor is of marble, and there is a low fountain at the centre.

The corridor on the left is joined by that same dark, narrow passageway which allowed the king to reach the vestibule when

The Cuarto del Príncipe.
Right ceiling.

he was in danger without needing to cross the main area. On the right at the end of this corridor is the entrance to the **Cuarto del Príncipe** ("Room of the Prince").

F) The Cuarto del Príncipe

The Cuarto del Príncipe ("Room of the Prince") was named in memory of the Catholic Kings' son and heir, Prince John, who was born in the Alcázar in 1478. He died very young, thus dashing hopes of a direct succession to the Spanish throne. Isabella and Ferdinand's successor was finally to be their grandson, Charles of Habsburg. John died of his "love of love"; as the epitaph on his grave poetically tells us, he: "Died of love's ills".

This room is set out like those in the palace in Granada, i.e with a central area flanked on both sides by a bed-chamber reached through beautiful arches. Through an opening which illuminates the whole room in a most extraordinary manner, the left chamber leads directly to the **garden,** also known as the Jardín del Príncipe ("Garden of the Prince"). The central room has a window, built later than the others, overlooking the **Patio de la Montería** ("Court of the Hunt"). So as to distinguish it from the rest of the ornamentation in the room, the stuccowork around it was not coloured. Characteristically, the original ornamentation takes the form of friezes running around the walls below the ceiling. Here, however, the ornamentation forms multifoil arches on small columns, interlacing motifs and Kufic inscriptions, all highly coloured. The faces of the openings and the latticed depressions above the main door also display stuccowork with geometric and vegetal motif decoration.

Of special interest in these rooms are the **beautiful ceilings.** The one in the main room is rectangular, like the ground plan, and flat. It

The Cuarto del Príncipe.

The Cuarto del Príncipe. Left ceiling.

displays highly gilded and coloured interlacing patterns forming twelve-pointed stars combined with polygonal coffers with stalactite-work decoration.

The ceilings of the two **side bedrooms** are different from each other in shape. The one on the right is octagonal and rests on squinches adorned with stalactite-work decoration. It displays interlacing motifs and the frieze is painted with the heraldic motifs of the Castilian monarchy. The whole ceiling has been greatly altered. The left bedroom, built in 1543 by the Alcázar's head carpenter, Juan de Simancas, contains one of the finest examples of Renaissance ceilings. Simancas's name and the date are featured in a cartouche on the supporting frieze on the rear wall, as is the year of the room's most recent restoration (1834). This flat, square, richly painted **ceiling** is made up of coffers all the same shape displaying interlacing work with various designs around pine-cone prisms and divided up by moulding imitating Plateresque balusters. The **frieze** is decorated with human and animal figures facing each other and supporting shields, thus constituting an example of the purest Plateresque so typical of early Spanish Renaissance architecture.

The floor as it is today is the result of very recent restoration work, the original having been transferred to rooms in the Upper Palace in order to avoid deterioration due to use by the public.

In the Mudéjar palace this area would in all likelihood have been the queen's room. When Isabella the Catholic was in residence in the palace, these rooms became the summer apartments; consequently winter chambers were built for her in the same section on the floor above. These are reached by a staircase behind the door in the west wall, close to the opening which leads out into the garden.

G) The Cuarto del Techo de los Reyes Católicos

To the right after the Patio de las Muñecas and at the end of the gallery in this area stands this square room known as the Cuarto del Techo de los Reyes Católicos ("Room of the Ceiling of the Catholic Kings"). Its position is symmetrical to that of the Cuadra de Pasos Perdidos and, like it, the room has a **very beautiful ceiling,** which, as it was built during the reign of the Catholic Kings, was given this name. The ceiling displays interlacing designs which form a sort of broad band around a central pattern with a gilded pine-cone of prisms. All of this rests on a frieze bearing the heraldry of Isabella and Ferdinand – the yoke and arrows and the motto "Tanto Monta", which described the equal power of the two monarchs who unified the two Spanish kingdoms. Also very beautiful are the stucco decoration around the top of the walls, the frames of the doorway leading to the adjacent room, and the *ajimez* or geminated window overlooking the **Jardín del Príncipe** ("Garden of the Prince").

Another important feature of this room is the clay and tile paving with its extremely beautiful glazed ceramics skirting. It is one of the few remaining original floors in the palace.

H) The Salón del Techo de Felipe II

A door in the left wall leads to the Salón del Techo de Felipe II ("Hall of the Ceiling of Philip II"), a long room named after its ceiling, which was built between 1589 and 1591 during the reign of Philip the Prudent. Designed by Martín Infante, the Alcázar's head carpenter at

(Right) The Arco de los Pavones in the Salón del Techo de Felipe II.

(Left) The Salón del Techo de Felipe II. The ceiling.

that time, the ceiling is made up of square coffers whose inner faces are carved with very Renaissance-style geometric designs possibly inspired by those of Serlio. It rests on a **frieze of brackets** and was gilded and painted entirely by Baltasar de Bracamonte, a contemporary painter. Due to its shape this room was also known as

Detail from the Arco de los Pavones.

the **Sala de la Media Caña** ("Room of the Coving"). Both the room and the ceiling are the longest in the palace.

A door in the right wall leads to the Jardín del Príncipe. This exit is flanked by two small *ajimeces* or geminated windows which allow a great deal of light to enter, thus accentuating the room's profuse decoration.

Particularly important here is the **Arco de los Pavones** ("Arch of the Peacocks"), in reference to the birds which adorn it. This leads to the Mudéjar palace's most important room – the **Salón de Embajadores** ("Hall of Ambassadors").

This arch was the original point of access to the hall when it formed part of Al-Muwarak's Abbadid palace (11th century), which was oriented towards the west.

The composition is an extremely solemn one in which a large, very depressed, horseshoe arch frames a Cordovan-type triple arch resting on columns with beautiful dark shafts; these are surmounted with two gilded capitals, one caliphal, the other Renaissance. Above this are the typical small latticed windows which, as we have seen, are a constant feature of the architecture of this palace, as they are in the Alhambra and Madinat al-Zahra. Also very interesting is the extremely beautiful painted and gilded stucco decoration, and above all the figures of birds, not only the lovely peacocks mentioned above but also the frieze which displays a group of birds of prey, including eagles and hawks in various attitudes and on vegetal backgrounds forming circles. These motifs were copied from gifts of cloth made by ambassadors from countries in the Far East to Peter I at his court in Seville.

The Arco de los Pavones entrance.

The Salón de Embajadores.

As in all the other halls in the palace, the walls here display high tiled friezes with interlacing patterns surmounted with merlon bands.

On the right-hand side at the back of this room, a door leads to the **Salas de Infantes** ("Rooms of the Infantes"). Flanking the **Arco de los Pavones,** two other doors lead to the side bedrooms of the **Salón de Embajadores.**

I) Salón de Embajadores

The square Salón de Embajadores ("Hall of Ambassadors") the **richest and most spectacular room in the complex,** was the

Detail from the balcony locks.

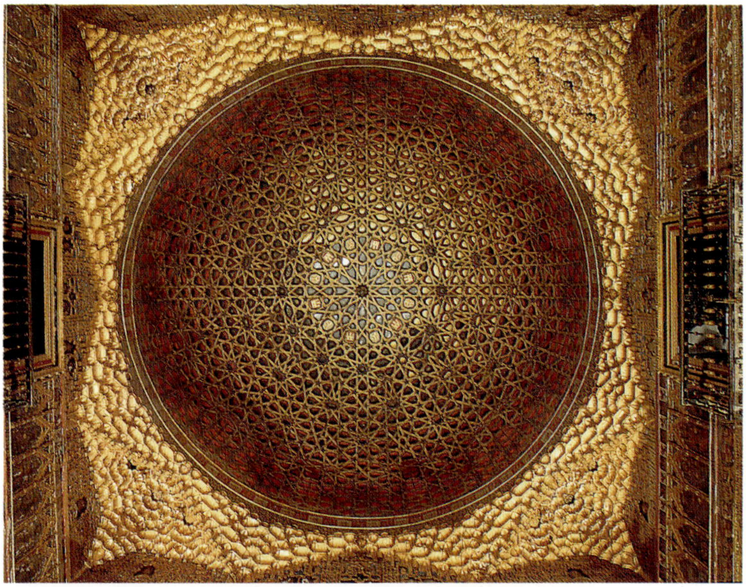

The dome in the Salón de Embajadores.

Detail from the Salón de Embajadores.

Mudéjar palace's throne room. Due to its dome the palace records refer to it as the **Sala de la Media Naranja** ("Room of the Dome"). It is flanked on either side by rectangular bedrooms.

Three of the walls of the main room contain triple, Cordovan-style horseshoe arches. These are framed by larger recessed arches whose layout is extraordinarily reminiscent of those in the rich hall of the Cordovan palace of Madinat al-Zahra. Particularly interesting are the columns, whose dark pink shafts are surmounted with gilded caliphal

Stuccowork decoration in the Salón de Embajadores.

(Left) The Salón de Embajadores. Doors.
(Right) The Salón de Embajadores. Friezes.

capitals. The archway leading to the Patio de las Doncellas dates from the 14th century, when the builders took advantage of this old Muslim **Throne Room** and constructed Peter's new palace around it. The ceiling is a fabulous wooden dome decorated with interlacing designs forming stars and symbolising the universe. It is not the original dome, however, for it was built, as an inscription on it confirms, by the royal carpenter Diego Roiz in 1427 during the reign of John II.

The Salón de Embajadores. Arches.

Everything in this room is a faithful reproduction of the great *qubba* in the Cordovan palace of Madinat al-Zahra. However, the magnificent **stucco decoration** which covers the walls entirely with geometric patterns, diamond-pattern panels and vegetal motifs and the Kufic inscriptions surrounding the panels date

The Salas de Infantes.

from the 14th and 15th centuries. The magnificent tiled friezes, with a variety of geometric designs, also date from the 14th century. The colour and gilding accentuate the richness and sumptuousness of this fabulous room.

The splendid **Puertas de Gorroneras** ("Pivoting Doors") also belong to the Mudéjar period. Dating from 1366, they are of painted inlaid wood and display different interlacing designs on each side. Without any doubt they are the finest in the palace and are considered jewels of Toledo carpentry.

In the 16th century (1592-1597), four balconies were built into the upper walls of this room to connect it with the chambers in the Upper Palace. The wrought iron work, by Francisco López, is considered among the most important of its kind in the Alcázar. From the same period is the gallery of kings painted on the frieze and framed by small Gothic chapels. These portraits, by Diego de Esquivel and executed between 1599 and 1600, depict the Spanish monarchs from Recceswinth to Philip III. Esquivel also painted the **thirty-two busts of ladies** in the area above this

The ceiling in the Salón del Techo de Carlos V.

frieze (1598), and may have been responsible for all the pictorial ornamentation in the upper areas, in which the symbols of the Spanish monarchy in general and those of each king in particular are featured.

To **either side** of this room is a rectangular, symmetrically arranged **bedroom** with a wooden ceiling displaying geometric forms. These date from between 1590 and 1598 and replaced the original ones. They have been ascribed to Martín Infante, then head carpenter. Both rooms have friezes around the upper walls. Made by Gothic masters, they display silhouettes of human and animal figures and vine, oak, ilex and fig leaves. One room faces the Patio de las Muñecas and the other the Salas de Infantes.

J) The Salas de Infantes

The Salas de Infantes ("Rooms of the Infantes"), which is symmetrical to the area known as the Cuarto del Príncipe ("Room of the Prince") in the north section, consists of a main room and two side rooms. Although it is also called the **Comedor** ("Dining-room"), it was originally the chambers of the Infantes. A great number of changes have been made to this area: the original floors have been replaced and the painted elements, particularly the stucco decoration and ceilings, have been restored in a rather peculiar way with loud colours.

From the central room, in which, according to an inscription on the wall, María Isabel de Orleans Borbón was born in 1848, a corridor leads to the **Jardín de la Galera** ("Garden of the Galley").

K) The Salón del Techo de Carlos V

At the end of the Salas de Infantes lies the palace's old chapel, now known as the **Salón del Techo de Carlos V** ("Room of the Ceiling of Charles V") – a reference to the ceiling built (1541-1542) during the reign of the emperor and ascribed to master carpenter Sebastián de Segovia.

The fact that this room was used as a chapel is confirmed at the entrance by an inscription in monastic Gothic script which contains a well-known prayer from the Eucharist: "Passion of Christ, comfort me. Water of the side of Christ, cleanse me; etc."

The entrance, a semi-circular archway, is surmounted with small latticed windows and framed by rich stucco panels with epigraphic vegetal and geometric motifs; the decoration also bedecks the small geminated windows on either side of the door. These windows have shutters of gilded and coloured inlaid wood of the same type as those in the other halls. This area consists

(Facing page)
The Salón del Techo de Carlos V.

of a **room** and a **bedroom** divided by a beautiful semi-circular arch resting on small columns surmounted with caliphal capitals. Lovely stuccoed **friezes** adorn the walls in the space above the tilework and below the ceiling with alternating interlacing motifs, Kufic inscriptions and Castilian heraldry. The original floor has been replaced.

Particularly important in this room is the **ceiling** – one of the most beautiful in the palace. It consists of polygonal and smaller diamond-shaped coffers within beautiful Classical mouldings. At the centre of the former are rosettes which alternate with beautiful, extremely Classical busts of ladies and gentlemen both young and old. The ceiling, which replaced the original Mudéjar one, rests on a frieze, also of wood, carved with alternating imperial heraldic symbols – the coat of arms with the two-headed eagle and the pillars. During the Renaissance this room was dubbed the **Sala Nueva Baja** ("New Lower Room") or **Sala de los Artesones** ("Room of the Coffers").

Although the Upper Palace is not open to the public, some of its most outstanding features should at least be mentioned.

Signed and dated by the Italian Niculoso Pisano in 1504, the **altar and altarpiece** of the Oratorio de los Reyes Católicos ("Oratory of the Catholic Kings") is not only a Renaissance masterpiece but was also the first of its kind to be made in Seville with the flat coloured-tile technique (later widely imitated). Framed by beautiful bands with grotesques, the scene in the centre depicts the Virgin visiting her cousin Elizabeth. The frontal displays the heraldry and initials of the Catholic Kings, a Classical laurel wreath around a scene of the *Annunciation,* and Plateresque figures and symbols, all executed impeccably and in beautiful strong, vibrant colours typical of 15th-century Tuscan ceramics. The **chapel** it dominates was the Catholic Queen's private oratory and forms part of the **Cuarto de la Reina** ("Room of the Queen").

The room is small but its beauty is great. Indeed, it is an architectural jewel. Standing on a rectangular plan, it is divided into three by two central marble columns supporting prism-covered capitals surmounted with extremely beautiful ogee mouldings with gilded oak leaves. These support basket-handle arches, the second ones being adorned with a Gothic clerestory and vegetal decoration supported by wall brackets in *culs de lampe* which reproduce the adornment on the capital.

The ribs of the **Gothic vaults** over the two sections also spring from these supports. The keystones are adorned with the Catholic Kings' initials: F. and Y.

These structures produce a Moorish notion of space as interpreted in the Gothic manner and form a delicate, extraordinarily exquisite whole.

The Oratorio de los Reyes Católicos in the Upper Palace.

The Sala de Audiencias.

Also important in the Upper Palace are certain rooms considered its most distinguished chambers. These include the **Antechamber,** the **Sala de Audiences** ("Audience Room") or **Cámara Real Alta** ("Upper Royal Chamber") and the **Despacho del Rey** ("Office of the King"). In the 16th century, they were known together as the **Cuarto de Hércules** ("Room of Hercules") and the **Cuarto de las Cinco Cuadras** ("Room of the Five Halls"). The **Cámara Real** ("Royal Chamber") and the **Dormitorio del Rey Don Pedro** ("Bedroom of King Peter"), which are the most solemn of them all, were the only Mudéjar rooms built in the Upper Palace during the 14th century. The latter, which is rectangular in shape, stands in the centre of the Upper Palace and has a narrow three-arched corridor which delimits the row of windows overlooking the Patio de la Montería.

Other adornments in this room are a number of embedded wall arches, those in the middle and surrounding the entrances to the other rooms being larger than those at the sides, which are of different widths and rest on columns with alternating pink, black and white marble shafts surmounted with reused gilded caliphal capitals.

The **walls** display tilework friezes dating from the time of the room's construction, while a low stonework ledge or bench covered in ceramics runs all around the room. The remaining sections of the walls up to the ceiling are decorated with lovely Mudéjar vegetal motif **stuccowork,** interlacing designs, stalactite-work, inscriptions and the heraldry of the Kings of Castile, all very beautifully coloured and gilded. The splendid **ceiling** is of interlacing designs. The floor, of clay and tiling, is the original one.

This, the most solemn room of those in the Upper Palace, is preceded by the **Antechamber** and leads to the **Despacho del Rey**, which is divided into two sections by a very caliphal-looking triple arch resting on Renaissance marble columns with gilded capitals. These rooms afford one of the best views of the cathedral with the Giralda, its lovely tower, at its side.

IX. THE PATIO DEL CRUCERO OR PATIO DE DOÑA MARÍA DE PADILLA

To the right from the Patio de la Montería, an 18th-century gallery leads to the Apeadero ("Alighting-place"). Approximately halfway along this gallery, a door, also dating from the 18th century, leads to the **Patio de Doña María de Padilla** ("Court of Doña María de Padilla").

The Baños de Doña María de Padilla.

This court is a **square** with vegetation at each corner delimited by myrtle hedges. Originally (12th century) this was an Almohad "crossing place" on two levels, the upper one consisting of four platforms converging at the centre and another around the edges. These platforms were supported by pillars and vaults; in the middle of the court was a pool.

Alterations were made to this garden in the mid-13th century, when Alfonso X erected the Gothic palace – now the Salones de Carlos V – which overlooks it.

In the wake of the tragic Lisbon earthquake, which damaged so many of the Alcázar's buildings, a great deal of work was carried out on the court in the 18th century. As part of this work, the **Neo-Classical Corridor** (designed by the engineer Sebastián van der Borcht), in front of the Salones, was built.

X. THE SALONES DE CARLOS V

This is now the name ("Halls of Charles V") of the halls which comprise the Gothic palace erected by Alfonso X the Wise in the mid-13th century on the site of the old Almohad palace. In the Middle Ages, this palace was also known as the **Cuarto del**

The Salones de Carlos V. The Chapel.

The Salones de Carlos V.
The Chapel. Picture of the Virgin of the Kings between St Hermenegild and St Ferdinand.

Caracol ("Room of the Spiral Staircase"), an allusion to the stairs in the towers at each corner. The walls of these towers were finished with merlons, features which at least outwardly still exist. This was the residence of María de Padilla, after whom the court preceding these halls – in which Alfonso X the Wise's court assembled – was named.

Although the original layout has been preserved, the palace is now greatly changed and comprises two large rectangular halls

The Salones de Carlos V. Room next to the gardens. Detail from tilework by Cristóbal de Augusta.

lying parallel to the court plus another two, smaller ones, at right angles to them. Except for the first of these, known as the **Salón de Tapices** ("Hall of Tapestries"), all have preserved their stout Gothic groined vaults (built by stonemasons from Burgos), although the original Gothic austerity is concealed by Renaissance motifs added between 1577 and 1583. During this period the large windows which overlook the garden were built, thus filling these dark halls with light. Moreover, the lower portions of the walls were faced with very beautiful tilework friezes by the Sicilian Cristóbal de Augusta, paying homage with Renaissance themes to the Emperor Charles and the Empress Isabella, whose wedding banquet was held here; this is why the rooms are known not only as the **Salas de las Bóvedas** ("Rooms of the Vaults") but also as the **Salas de las Fiestas** ("Rooms of the Festivities").

The next hall is known as the **Salón de Tapices** because of the magnificent tapestries draping its walls. These include scenes from the conquest of Tunis, one of the emperor's greatest military campaigns. They were first painted by Jean de Vermayen and then transferred to tapestry (1535-1554) by Guillermo Pannemaker. This room is now almost totally remodelled and displays a large number of mouldings and decorative elements which it originally did not contain.

The chapel, containing a Siena-style altarpiece of the Virgin of La Antigua, is situated to the right. Of the numerous paintings adorning its walls, particularly interesting is the very recently researched **Adoration of the Shepherds,** painted in Granada in 1639 by Juan Leandro de la Fuente. An extremely Baroque work not without beauty, its colour, chiaroscuro and fluent brush-strokes reveal Venetian influence.

Also worthy of mention is the ***Virgin of Kings between St Hermenegild and St Ferdinand,*** painted by Domingo Martínez in 1740 for the *Palacio Real del León del Grullo* and, like the previous picture, only recently documented.

The room which stands symmetrical to this one and is identical to it is known as the **Sala de la Cantarera** ("Room of the Pitcher

Tapestry of the Conquest of Tunis, Real Alcázar, Seville.

Shelf"). Like the former, it has beautiful 16th-century grilles. It now houses the **Alcázar Library.**

XI. THE GARDENS

Beyond the last of the Salones de Carlos V and on the right lies one of the most beautiful areas in the Alcázar – the Gardens.

Known as *Mary al-Fidda* ("Meadow of Silver"), this large space was originally a military esplanade with an oratory. Subsequently (12th century), the Almohads raised a wall to delimit a triangular area, thus dividing the esplanade into two. This wall, which still stands, also served as a division for two areas containing gardens – the inner one next to the palace buildings, the outer beyond the Alcázar walls.

During the Islamic period the first area consisted of gardens, yards and a larger area containing the original oratory or *qubba,* whose name, given to the area known since then as the **Jardín de la Alcoba** ("Garden of the Bedroom"), was used until the Modern Age. It was here where, in successive phases throughout the 16th and 17th centuries, the oldest gardens in the Alcázar were built. Although these retained their original Arabic arrangement into compartments, they were treated according to the Italian Mannerist notion of aesthetics. Despite the fact that many of the original elements of these gardens have been lost, there are enough left to help us imagine their former greatness.

During the Modern Age, the area behind the wall was known as the **Jardín del Parque** ("Garden of the Park") and later as the **Retiro** ("Withdrawal"). It was laid out as a garden during this century.

Detail of the fountain in the Jardín del Estanque de Mercurio.

A) The Jardín del Estanque de Mercurio

The Jardín del Estanque de Mercurio ("Garden of the Pool of Mercury") is a quadrilateral area containing the pool and fountain of the god Mercury, from which it takes its name. The very beautiful statue was made by Diego de Pesquera and cast by Bartolomé de Morel; Pesquera and Morel also made the four small lions with shields and the globes surmounted with pyramids, all of bronze and subsequently gilded. The work was carried out between 1576 and 1577, as is recorded on the bases supporting the lions at each corner. The turned iron **handrails** around the pool (which was transformed into a Renaissance fountain) were also made during this period.

On the east side of the garden is the extremely beautiful **Galería del Grutesco** ("Gallery of the Grotto"), designed by Vermondo Resta.

The Jardín del Estanque de Mercurio.

Between 1612 and 1613 this architect masked the old wall and built its first section in the form of a triumphal arch, subsequently (1613-1621) laying out the rest as a series of *miradors*. All was originally painted in fresco with allegorical and mythological themes depicting the extraordinary wealth of 16th-century Seville, "Port and Gateway of the Indies", and centre of the monopoly on trade with the Americas.

Of great interest on the south side are the stonework benches which offer the visitor an opportunity to rest and admire the beauty of the garden. The front wall has a lovely high *mirador*, also by Vermondo Resta (1612).

B) The Jardín de las Danzas

An 18th-century staircase leads to the rectangular Jardín de las Danzas ("Garden of Dances"), which is laid out on two levels, the first containing marble columns and the second an extremely beautiful polygonal tile-covered fountain with a lovely 16th-century bronze-work spout.

The paths in this second section contain **hidden spouts** which – very much in line with Mannerist tastes – playfully spurt jets of water. This area also contains stonework benches covered with Seville tiling.

The Jardín de las Danzas.

The Baños de Doña María de Padilla.

The name of the garden comes from the myrtle bushes shaped into figures of nymphs and satyrs in the 16th and 17th centuries. Hands and heads of wood or painted baked clay were added to these so that the figures seem to be dancing together among the myrtle. This area also contains orange trees (close to the surrounding walls), myrtle hedges, tall rubber plants and a number of other plants added at a later time.

C) The Jardín del Crucero or Baños de Doña María de Padilla

To the right of the Jardín de las Danzas is the vaulted entrance to the very old Jardín del Crucero or Baños de Doña María de Padilla ("Garden of the Crossing" or "Baths of Doña María de Padilla"). Originally (12th century) this was a rectangular Almohad **garden** with intersecting paths. It stood on two levels, the upper one, forming what is now the Patio de Doña María de Padilla, had three walkways, two of which intersected, while the third ran around the edges. This upper level was supported by pillared vaults and in the centre was a pool. In the four corners orange trees rose to the level of the upper walkways. This garden was part of the Almohad palace on whose site Alfonso X erected his Gothic palace in the middle of the 13th century. It remains intact but was reinforced with Gothic groined vaults.

In the 16th century (1578) a **"grotto fountain"** adorned with figures was built at the back of the garden at the end of the pool. Its walls were painted in fresco as were the vaults, which were later decorated with the signs of the zodiac. In

The gallery on the left in the Jardín de Troya.

this manner, the mediaeval garden was adapted to Renaissance tastes.

In the 18th century, the garden's structures were seriously damaged in the Lisbon earthquake and it was necessary to reinforce them up to the level of the upper platforms. In more recent times, the old garden has recovered part of its original appearance. It was named after Doña María de Padilla, that lady who lived in the Gothic palace and was wooed and loved by Peter the Cruel.

D) The Jardín de Troya

From the Jardín de las Danzas a door on the right leads to a lower level and the **Jardín de Troya** ("Garden of Troy").

Its name comes from a stone maze with which the garden was paved in the 16th century but which was replaced by the present brick and tile path. At the centre is a lovely polygonal fountain.

The Jardín de las Flores. The fountain with remains of clay figures.

Particularly interesting here is the **corridor** on the left leading to the Jardín de las Damas ("Garden of the Ladies"). Built by the architect Vermondo Resta in 1606, it was covered with rough ashlars, had human heads on the capitals and pilasters, and was originally painted in fresco. A raised path runs above this corridor. Starting from the Jardín del Estanque, it leads to another garden at the end, known as the **Jardín de las Flores** ("Garden of Flowers"), passing over the wall dividing this first line of gardens and the second. From here, there is a lovely view of the whole complex.

The Jardín de las Flores. The frontispiece-niche.

E) The Jardín de la Galera

A semi-circular arch in the wall leads to a rectangular garden. Here, there are four large flower beds surrounded by myrtle hedges.

The garden's name ("Garden of the Galley") comes from galleys cut out of myrtle bushes in the 17th century which shot jets of water at each other in a mock naval battle.

In the wall next to the palace there is a gallery covered by a metal structure in the manner of a pergola. Here 16th-century stone pedestals with bas-reliefs of female dancers and grotesques, belonging to a corridor which once existed on the site, are kept.

F) The Jardín de las Flores

An arch in the back wall of the Jardín de la Galera leads to the next garden, the Jardín de las flores ("Garden of the Flowers"). Between two of the walls there is a rectangular fountain with the remains of a **grotto** of hollow stone and with baked-clay figures. The sides of the fountain are lined with beautiful tiling (now rather spoilt) made with the flat coloured-tile technique brought to Seville from Italy by Niculoso Pisano.

On the west side is a very Mannerist **frontispiece-niche,** ascribed to Vermondo Resta. It frames the remains of what was

The Jardín de las Damas, the large Grotto

The Jardín de las Damas.

once a grotto and fountain made between 1589 and 1601 which was adorned with a profusion of beautifully coloured figures, shells, snails, mother-of-pearl and other objects associated with the sea, all brought from the nearby coast of Cadiz. Today the structure contains a bust, probably of the emperor. In one of the brick pathways there is a small Arabic-style fountain and some of the vegetation among the myrtle hedges is very tall.

The Fuente de Neptuno.

G) The Jardín del Príncipe

To reach the Jardín del Príncipe ("Garden of the Prince") it is necessary to walk back to the Jardín de la Galera, take a corridor next to the palace wall and turn left. Although this garden – the last in this first section – is the **oldest**, it has been completely remodelled. Its name recalls the Catholic Kings' first child, Prince John, who was born in one of the rooms overlooking it.

The garden contains a **corridor** (also known as "of the Prince") built at the end of the 16th century (1589-1595) by Lorenzo de Quiedo, the Alcázar's master mason. It comprises two superimposed semi-circular arches on marble columns, the upper area being enclosed with modern glazing, although the original wooden **ceilings** (both dated), which have been ascribed to the master carpenter Martín Infante, still exist.

The second corridor, on the south side, was built by the architect Rafael Manzano Martos in 1976. It has intersecting brick walkways and a small, modern fountain. Plants grow in four areas surrounded by myrtle hedges and there are a number of palm trees.

The Jardín de las Damas.
The Galería del Grutesco.

The Jardín de las Damas.
The Gateway to the Jardín del Cenador.

H) The Jardín de las Damas

Rectangular in shape, the Jardín de las Damas ("Garden of the Ladies") is one of the largest in the old section. Designed and laid out with all its ornamentation by the Milanese architect Vermondo Resta (mentioned above), it became the most beautiful and modern **Mannerist garden** in the Spain of the Austrias. Begun in 1606, it was completed in 1624 in readiness for a visit to Seville by Philip IV.

The surrounding wall contains Italian-style, very Mannerist gateways and windows as well as **grottoes** in which figures of clay and lead once illustrated a number of mythological themes. The largest grotto contained a water-powered organ whose notes were produced by the pressure of the water. The brick and tile pathways contain a number of hidden **water spouts** which produce lovely combinations, and visitors – captivated by the beauty of the garden – are often taken by surprise.

Three fountains are situated at pathway intersections – two low Arabic-style ones near the edges of the garden, and another, very beautiful one, in the centre. Made of marble and originally from Genoa, the latter is surmounted with a bronze statue of Neptune, god of the sea (in a rather unnatural position) and is an imitation of a fountain made for the city of Bologna by Giovanni da Bologna.

One of the garden's most important features is the **Galería del Grotesco** ("Gallery of the Grotto"), which, as a series of *miradors*, runs along the east side to continue through the adjacent gardens. It was built between 1613 and 1621 by Vermondo Resta, who used bossed volcanic stone to imitate nature with a clearly Mannerist technique. All the columns of these tall ***miradors*** were brought in from different parts of the palace, and include a number of beautiful caliphal capitals in various styles. From the *miradors*, which have iron railings painted a deep blue, there is a fine view of the Real Alcázar's grounds. Like the walls, gateways and grottoes, the gallery was painted with frescoes imitating marble and foliage and depicting scenes from Classical mythology, all gilded and in beautiful colour. The result was a refined area having nothing to do with the rather rustic-looking garden as it stands today.

Nor was the vegetation in this garden as tall as it is now; originally the plants which grew here accentuated the garden's geometric layout and formed motifs from the heraldry of the Spanish monarchy.

Finally, the **entrance gates** were guarded by the figures of Hercules and Antaeus wrestling, their bodies formed by vegetation and their hands and heads of wood or clay. Like so many of this garden's ornamental features, these have been lost with the passing of time. In spite of all this, however, the garden has retained some of that distinction which once made it an example to follow for Sevillian Renaissance landscape gardeners.

I) The Jardín de la Cruz

This garden stands on the west side of the Jardín de las Damas. Jardín de la Cruz ("Garden of the Cross") was its original name in the 16th century, but around 1626 it became known as the **Jardín del Laberinto** ("Garden of the Labyrinth"), in reference to the magnificent myrtle maze (with a polygonal pond in the centre

The Jardín de la Cruz. The pool and mountain.

The Cenador de Carlos V.

and a "mountain" in the form of a grotto) which covered most of the area.

Although the maze is now lost, the **pond** and **mountain** still exist, albeit in a bad state of repair and divested of most of their ornamental figures. These formed a scene with Mount Parnassus presided over by Apollo surrounded by the nine muses, all surmounted by the horse Pegasus raising the fountain Hippocrene with his foot.

The whole garden complex was a recreation of the **myth of Daedalus.** Visible today are the large lead pipes through which the water circulated – leaping from side to side as if actually rising from the entrails of the earth – and the remains of clay heads (various animal heads and one human) on the mountaintop.

All the trees and plants in this garden are tall and were planted at the beginning of this century.

J) The Jardín del Cenador de la Alcoba

This garden takes its name from the old oratory in the area known as the **Huerta de la Alcoba** ("Garden of the Bedroom") which was converted (1543-1546) into a *cenador* (a bower or garden pavilion) in

The Jardín del Cenador de la Alcoba.
The Cenador de Carlos V.

The Cenador de Carlos V. A window in the interior.

The Cenador de Carlos V. Tiling on the exterior.

The Cenador del León. Detail of the remains of frescoes in the interior.

The Cenador del León and the pool.

the times of the emperor. Since then it has been known as the **Cenador de Carlos V** ("Bower of Charles V"). It consists of a square building with a gallery of semi-circular arches resting on each side on marble columns. Made in Genoa, these columns probably came from the Aprille de Carona workshops. In front of the building are tiled stonework benches.

Both inside and out, the **walls** display the same type of ceramics – made in the Polido brothers' workshops in Triana – although in

The Puerta del Privilegio.

The Jardín de los Poetas. The pools.

the upper sections there is Mudéjar (exterior) and Plateresque (interior) stuccowork.

Particularly interesting is the extremely beautiful design of the **paving,** a combination of clay and glazed ceramics which includes the date of the work and the name of its author, the Alcázar's head mason Juan Fernández. All of this can be seen in the far corners. In the centre is a beautiful **low marble fountain** with a small channel, also of marble, which takes water to the corridor outside, thus cooling the whole area. The building is surrounded by square flower beds with box-hedge borders.

Opposite is another pavilion known as the **Pabellón del León** ("Pavilion of the Lion"), an allusion to the statue standing above its pool. This beautiful building constructed in 1645 by the Alcázar's head mason Diego Martín Orejuela, was one of the last works executed in the Seville Mannerist style.

Both the interior and exterior were originally painted in fresco; what remains of this decoration has recently been restored (1991). Judging by the frescoes – by Juan de Medina – this would seem to have been a pavilion dedicated to Love.

The Jardín del Marqués de La Vega Inclán. Detail from a fountain and pool.

Towards the front on one side of this garden, a myrtle maze has been planted in an attempt to copy the Alcázar's old labyrinth.

K) The New Gardens

The solemn gateway of the Puerta del Privilegio ("Gateway of Privilege") in the Galería del Grotesco (both by the architect Vermondo Resta), leads to a very large area of gardens once forming part of the Alcázar's outer grounds. Originally known as the Huerta del Parque ("Garden of the Park") it was subsequently renamed the Huerta del Retiro ("Garden of Withdrawal").

It was here where these gardens, begun at the beginning of the century by the Marquis of La Vega Inclán and completed by Gómez Millán, were laid out. Of interest in this area is the **Jardín Inglés** ("English Garden"), which is arranged like a meadow and whose west side surrounds the Old Gardens.

In the south-east section is the **Jardín de los Poetas** ("Garden of the Poets"), which is arranged in the style of a Romantic garden. At its centre are two beautiful pools with columns at one end; the pools are delimited by box hedges flanking a small fountain.

Next to this stands the **Jardín del Marqués de la Vega Inclán** ("Garden of the Marquis of La Vega Inclán"), a Sevillian garden characterised by features typical of the Renaissance, to which Granada-style fountains and pools were added. The flora in all this area is very tall.

The Puerta de Marchena.

At the beginning of this century the rest of the Huerta del Retiro was ceded to the city, and the **Jardines de Catalina de Ribera** ("Gardens of Catalina de Ribera"), commonly known as the Jardines de Murillo ("Gardens of Murillo"), were created within it. These are separated from the Alcázar by a fence which was built at the time of their construction.

At the end of the Jardín del Marqués de la Vega Inclán is a **Gothic portal** dating from the time of the Catholic Kings. It came from the palace of the Duke of Arcos de Marchena and was purchased at an auction by Alfonso XIII. It was placed next to the beautiful **Torre del Enlace** ("Tower of the Liaison") by the Marquis of La Vega Inclán himself. This portal leads to another group of old gardens (situated between the palace buildings and the old wall), and on to the **Apeadero** ("Alighting-place").

XII. THE LAST SECTION OF THE OLD GARDENS

This fringe is now made up of two gardens, although in the 16th century there were four – the Jardín del Chorrón, the Jardín del Cidral, the Jardín del Alcubilla and the Jardín del Conde.

The **Puerta de Marchena** ("Marchena Portal") leads to a rectangular area of little interest, except perhaps for recently discovered remains, on the right and in the middle of the old wall, of an old channel which once carried water to these gardens. This is the garden once known as the Jardín del Chorrón.

The entrance to the Apeadero. Ceramic coat of arms of Philip V.

At the back stands the **Pabellón de la China** ("Pavilion of China"), which divides this area from the adjacent garden, known as the **Jardín de la Alcubilla** ("Garden of the Reservoir"). Recently restored, the Pavilion was built in the 18th century and displays iron gratings and gates dating from the time when Philip V set up his court in the Alcázar. Philip's coat of arms is displayed on the tympanum of the pediment (with a triple inflection fronton) surmounting a doorway at the entrance. Here a passage running parallel to the gardens leads to the Apeadero.

The Jardín de la Alcubilla has intersecting pathways which form large square flowerbeds delimited at the corners by box trees. An extremely beautiful **fountain** in the centre, originally from the Palace of the Duke of Medina Sidonia, dates from the 16th century. In front of the old palace wall, which delimits one of its sides, are very ancient orange and lemon trees. At the back stands the old **Cuarto del Alcaide** ("Room of the Governor") building, connected to this garden by a beautiful corridor.

XIII. THE APEADERO

This is a very sober area laid out almost like a basilica which acts as an entrance to the palace and leads to the **Patio de las Banderas** ("Court of the Flags"). Designed by the architect Vermondo Resta, the Apeadero ("Alighting-place") was built between 1607 and 1609 in three sections, the central one being larger than those at the sides. These sections are divided up by semi-circular arches on beautiful paired marble Tuscan columns on pedestals standing at right angles

The Jardín de la Alcubilla.

to the walls. The walls contain engaged arches framed by pilasters. Mannerist-style mouldings adorn the whole of the area and the paving is of **Tarifa flags** at the sides and cobblestones laid out in geometric patterns in the centre. The ceilings are flat except in the last section, which is groined and was built in the 18th century.

Doors in this area lead to: the old **Cuarto del Sol** ("Room of the Sun"), also known as the **Cuarto del Alcaide** ("Room of the

Governor"); the **Cuarto del Maestre** ("Room of the Master"); the **Cuarto Alto** ("Upper Room") above the Apeadero, now used by the City Council as an exhibition room; and to the passage connecting it with the Patio de la Montería. On the wall at one end is a Baroque altarpiece with *The Presentation of the Virgin in the Temple*.

At the back is a very rich portal, also designed by Vermondo Resta and a jewel of Spanish Mannerist architecture. In the lower section above the entrance is a marble memorial tablet with the following inscription:

> Reigning in Spain Philip the Third,
> this work was constructed
> in the year MDCVII and was repaired,
> enlarged and employed as the Royal
> Armoury reigning Philip V
> in the year MDCCXXIX.

The entrance is surmounted with a large metal crown containing Philip V's coat of arms in tiling, and, below this, a tile inscription with the year of the building's last renovation.

The vault of the old armoury. Heraldry of Philip V and Isabella Farnese.

The Apeadero. The entrance from the Patio de las Banderas.

The Apeadero.

XIV. THE PATIO DE LAS BANDERAS

The Patio de las Banderas ("Court of the Flags") was the **Parade Ground** of the original fortified enclosure and centre of the Alcázar, the Dar al-Imara. It is surrounded by dwellings once used by Alcázar functionaries. The oldest wall runs along the north side, separating the Alcázar from what is now the Plaza del Triunfo (in the 16th century called the Plaza del Canto). Behind this rises the cathedral and its lovely tower, the Giralda, an extremely beautiful sight visible from the end of this court.

The centre, which is covered with *albero* soil, contains a beautiful fountain surrounded by a number of orange trees. In the south wall an arch leads to the **Callejón del Agua,** which runs alongside the Almohad wall. Here channels recently cleaned, reinforced and restored (1993) so that they are now perfectly transparent and beautifully lit, once brought water from Carmona to the Alcázar. On the other side of this passage lies the very popular Santa Cruz district.

BIBLIOGRAPHY

AMADOR DE LOS RÍOS, J. *Puertas del salón de embajadores del Alcázar de Sevilla.* "Museo Español de Antigüedades", Vol. III Madrid.

ANTUÑA, P. M. *Sevilla y sus monumentos árabes.* El Escorial, 1930.

BALLESTEROS BERETTA. "La Arquitectura Sevillana entre el Islam y Castilla". *Sevilla en el siglo XIII,* Sevilla, 1978.

BONET CORREA, A. "El Renacimiento y el Barroco en los jardines musulmanes españoles", *Cuadernos de La Alhambra,* 4, Granada, 1968.

BOSCH VILA, J. "La Sevilla Islámica, 712-1248", *Historia de Sevilla*, Sevilla, 1984.

CABEZA MÉNDEZ, J. Mª. *Real Alcázar Hispalense.* "Sevilla Agradecida", Sevilla, 1992.

—. *Restauración de las murallas de Sevilla.* "Arquitectura y ciudad". Madrid, 1993.

CARO, R. *Antigüedades y Principado de la Ilustrísima ciudad de Sevilla y corografía de su convento jurídico.* Sevilla, 1634, reimp. 1896, Vol. I.

CARRIAZO, J. de M. *La boda del Emperador.* Sevilla, 1959.

—. *El Alcázar de Sevilla.* Barcelona, 1930.

CHECA CREMADES, F. "El Arte Islámico y la imagen de la naturaleza en la España del siglo XVI". *Fragmentos*, 1. Madrid, 1984.

CONTRERAS, R. *La Alhambra de Granada, el Alcázar y la gran mezquita de Occidente*, Madrid, 1855.

FERNÁN CABALLERO. *El Alcázar de Sevilla*, 1862.

GARCÍA MERCADAL, J. *Viajes de extranjeros por España y Portugal*, Vol. I, Madrid, 1952.

GESTOSO Y PÉREZ, J. *Sevilla monumental y artística*, Vol. I-II, Sevilla, 1889.

GUERRERO LOVILLO, J. "Al-qars al Mubarak, el Alcázar de la bendición". *Bol de B. A.* 2ª época, 11. Sevilla, 1974.

JIMÉNEZ MARTÍN, A. "Jardines renacentistas y barrocos". *Gran Enciclopedia de Andalucía,* Vol. V, Sevilla, 1979.

LLAGUNO Y AMIROLA, E. *Noticias de los arquitectos y arquitectura de España desde su restauración*. Vols. I, II y IV. Con notas, adendas y documentos de J. A. Ceán Bermúdez, Reimp. Madrid, 1977.

LLEO CAÑAL, V. *Nueva Roma: Mitología y Humanismo en el Renacimiento sevillano*. Sevilla, 1979.

LOBATO DOMÍNGUEZ, J. y MARTÍN ESTEBAN A., "Dos pinturas inéditas del Patrimonio Nacional en los Reales Alcázares de Sevilla". *Reales Sitios,* 122, Madrid, 1994.

MANZANO MARTOS, R. "Arquitectura de la Sevilla

Medieval". *Breve Historia de la Arquitectura en Sevilla.* Sevilla, 1985.

Poetas y vida literaria en los Reales Alcázares de Sevilla. Sevilla, 1983.

"Reales Alcázares". *Museos de Sevilla.* Madrid, 1977.

MARÍN FIDALGO, A. "Obras en los Reales Alcázares en tiempos de Carlos V". *Archivo Hispalense,* 200. Sevilla, 1982.

"Los jardines del Alcázar de Sevilla en el quinientos". *Cuadernos de la Alhambra,* 24. Granada, 1989.

"Los jardines del Alcázar de Sevilla en el siglo XVII". *Cuadernos de la Alhambra,* 26. Granada, 1990.

El Alcázar de Sevilla bajo los Austrias. Estudio arquitectónico e histórico, Sevilla, 1990. Vols. I-II.

"Pintura de corte humanista en los jardines del Alcázar de Sevilla. Las decoraciones de los cenadores Ochavado y del León". *Archivo Español de Arte,* 254. Madrid, 1991.

"Los Reales Alcázares de Sevilla: digna morada de la realeza española". *Reales Sitios,* 111. Madrid 1992.

Guía de los Reales Alcázares de Sevilla. Sevilla, 1992.

MONTOTO, S. "La catedral y el Alcázar de Sevilla". *Los monumentos cardinales de España.* Madrid, 1951.

ROMERO MURUBE, J. *El Alcázar de Sevilla.* Madrid, 1977.

TORRES BALBAS. L. "Arte almohade, arte nazarí, arte mudéjar". *Ars Hispaniae,* Vol. IV. Madrid, 1949.

TUBINO, F. Mª. *El Arte en España.* Sevilla, 1886.

"Vermondo Resta". Arte Hispalense, 48. Sevilla, 1988.

This book, published by Aldeasa, was printed in Madrid
on 18th December 1998, feast of Our Lady of Expectation,
at Estudios Gráficos Europeos